CONTENTS

ACKNOWLEDGEMENTS

"Widow," © Copyright 1994, Tova Green, appeared in *Honoring Loss: Celebrating Life*, the newsletter of the Doves Tour of the Former Yugoslavia, June, 1994, as well as in *Turning Wheel*, the Buddhist Peace Fellowship newsletter, 1994.

"Petal Child," © Copyright 1994, Cora Greenhill, was published in the anthology *If Not a Mother* (U.K.: Clare Butler, 1994).

"Excerpt from a Letter to a Friend," © Copyright 1993, Lee Anne Grundish, appeared in *Perceptions*, 1993.

"Memory's Burden," © Copyright 1994, Fran Peavy, was published in *Honoring Loss: Celebrating Life*, the newsletter of the Doves Tour of the Former Yugoslavia, June, 1994.

"Did Someone Once?," © Copyright 1975, Jean Pumphrey, was published in *Sunbury*, 1975, and appeared in her collection of poems, *Sheltered at the Edge, 1981*.

"The Swallows of War," © Copyright 1994, Rhiannon, appeared in *Honoring Loss: Celebrating Life*, the newsletter of the Doves Tour of the Former Yugoslavia, June, 1994.

EDITORIAL

Janet M. McEwan

> *It is in our own personal stories that the real herstory of our time is told. This periodical is a place for exploring the boundaries of our empowerment to break long historical and personal silences. While honoring the writing which still needs to be held close to our hearts, we can begin to send some of our heartfelt words out into a wider circle.*

The call of spiritual Home at the edges of the sea draws me for this Winter issue to writing conjuring women and ocean and other waters. In these pages, women pray, become water, stand at the edge, dive deeply, cavort, grapple with vulnerabilty, reclaim wild visions, walk or sit in grief, and drink secrets.

With a daughter's "Swimming Back Through Lost Seas" to her father, and a young widow's healing beach walk, notice another theme beginning to unfold. In poems from "Crazed Cookies" to "Chili Beans," and "Bedbugs," surprising yet familiar images of grief arise. Daughters grieve for parents, a mother for a son, a doctor for a patient, a friend for a friend who died of AIDS, a mother for a lost unborn daughter. Look for echoing imagery: the need to say goodbye, healing through dream, swallows that dart in and out through the pages.

With Tova Green's "Widow" the grieving of widows merges into the grieving of war. I have the honor of sharing with you the poems of three extraordinary women who undertook a healing journey deep within the conflict of the former Yugoslavia, one of the places in our world where the number and magnitude of the losses are almost beyond the imagining of those of us who do not live where we "see bombed out houses/Troops at checkpoints" (Fran Peavy, "Memory's Burden," p. 42). Complementing their poems is another by Vesna Dye, a Yugoslavia native now living in California and reflecting on the pain of her original home. Gloria Dyc's "What They Knew" continues the reflection on war in a different landscape.

Look next for a varied and inspiring collection of pieces. Here are hints to intrigue you: one young woman's struggle to accept and honor what she sees as "other" within herself; a woman's escape from abuse; a momentous decision; two very young women, Juliana Neely, 13, and Brooke Silverbrand, 15, writing about their grandmothers; an irrevent and suspenseful birth tale; the saga of a courageous life; and a celebration of "The Writer." And more!

If the themes of this issue touch you, here are two worthy matters I invite you to support along with *Writing For Our Lives***:**

The **Sacred Grove Women's Forest Sanctuary**, is very close to that northern California coastal wilderness where "Running Deer" was born (see *WFOL* Spring/Summer, 1993, for the story). "The vision…is to raise the funds to purchase a beautiful old growth Redwood grove…in the name of women. The vision is to return the land to the land as an act of healing and reconciliation with nature and to create a ritual and meditation space where women and their allies can hear the wisdom of the ancient forest." Having helped form the non-profit organization and participated in ritual on the land, I can attest to its beauty and the "wild-her-ness" of the dream. Volunteers and any amount of contribution are welcome and needed. To join the circle of supporters, call Running Deer Press (408) 354-8604, or Women's Forest Sanctuary at (510) 548-1693.

The Doves are a group of ten women, artists, performers, and activists, eight from California, two from Malaysia, who spent over three weeks this summer visiting and entertaining women, men and children on all sides of the conflict in the former Yugoslavia. Throughout their tour, they were hosted by relief organizations and anti-war activists. They produced seven concerts and visited six refugee camps, where they gave workshops and listened to stories, based on their theme of "Honoring Loss/ Celebrating Life." If you would like to know what you can do to help the former Yugoslavia, or if your group would like to organize a talk, a performance, or a slide show with members of the Doves, contact them at (510) 428-0240.

WFOL enjoyed a successful first public reading event in September, at the ClaireLight Bookstore in Santa Rosa, CA. Ten *WFOL* contributors from the San Francisco Bay Area read their contributions before an enthusiastic audience at the popular women's bookstore. The event opened the way for more readings and events to come, in California and elsewhere. Your continued support helps make possible this dream of widening the circles of women's personal, silence-breaking, and healing words. Thanks for all the kind words, writings, and subscriptions you send.

PISCES WOMAN PRAYS

Christine Irving

Themis, Goddess,
Oracle Dolphin,
Sea Mother,
She-of-Water,
throughout this year
come, guide
your daughter.

Two crescent moons
Define a womb-
Fish,
born on combs
of floating spume;
siren scales
slide under wave
sounding an
unfathomed cave
finny bodies form
a rune
in sky bound leaps
against the moon
jaws agape
to swallow men,
transform,
and spit
them out again.

Themis, Goddess,
Oracle Dolphin,
Sea Mother,
She-of-Water,
throughout this year
come, guide
your daughter

OF THE SEA
Mia T. Starr

I am of the boundless blue sea
In which I covet the sun.
It is to search all that is peaceful.

I want to lay the tired hands that never cease to weave.
I want to walk the weary feet that race to the sky.
I want to unite the heart and mind fighting to lend to the
    emotions of love
      and to the emotions of rationale.
I want to rest the body in the serenity of infinity.

I am of the boundless blue sea
In which I embark the moon.
It is to shine into the night.

I fear the coldness trapping the soul of life.
I weep the tears of frustration.
I seek the meaning of a woman struggling for happiness.
I strangle the anger crashing on the shore of turmoil.
I rage a furious roar—only I alone can feel
For I am alone in the night.
I surrender…leaving only the traces of footprints in the sand.

I am of the boundless blue sea
In which I cover the earth.
It is to embrace all that can be.

I want to sail the high tides of hope.
I want to hear the wind soar for dreams.
I want to feel the brisk air of aspirations.
I want to catch the waves of power.
I want to breathe the soul that yearns for the vast open sea.

I am boundless and I am free.

DID SOMEONE ONCE?

Jean Pumphrey

Did someone once
knowing that sound first
through cypresses
stand alone
by the Pacific?

And did
that first one
stand alone
like a god
before such vastness
echoing wider
than any imaginable abyss?

And did she feel
a living rock
a naked god
above the rocks
stretching out like basking seals?

I stand here
before this pulsing deep
hearing other echoes
a thousand sounds
seeing dragons
shaped like airways
monsters
above the sea.

I see as I am
as was described to me.
Did someone once
by the Pacific
stand alone
taking in
this vastness breathing?

FROM A JOURNAL ENTRY
Eileen Storey

Tuesday, 23 March, 3:37 p.m.
This goes out to all sentient beings…
The Oregon Coast, Ecola State Park

My heart hasn't beaten since I stepped foot on the trail. And now I am on the zenith of a rock outcropping with a single spindly spruce to feel the beauty with me. My very own Bo tree. Below me is the lusty lap of the Pacific ocean, and above me a sky reaching farther than it ever could in Texas. Galveston—I shudder to think of what I used to think of as Ocean. The wind is fierce here, though, and I'm sure I look ridiculous all bundled up in coat, gloves, scarves, hat, and rubber boots that did nothing to stop the ocean from coming in, swirling icy around my toes. But how can I blame her? I dared her—stood there like a fool on the black pebble beach and said, "Pacific, I dare you to greet me!" And greet me she did. I'm soaked almost to my knees. It's about fifty-five degrees without the wind. Damn cold with wet feet, but I don't care, I'll stay here forever.

A man's climbing up my rock (*my* rock?) and now he's at the edge, where I was a minute ago. He's got his face to the sky, too. That's what you have to do up here, surrender to the sea, to the sky. You're such a wee thing between them. It's okay, him up here on the rock. He's quiet, reverent, and we are bodhisattvas together, beings sentient and small.

I love life now more than I have ever known. The ocean's cry rips my soul from my throat. And when her cold waters dark wash up with force through the blackrock beach, then pull back, there is the sound of a thousand hands clapping. It sounds like a car on gravel, these waves sucking back to the ocean.

My feet are soaking but ecstatic. They know the moment, too. Water birds ride the waves. The sun in the sky is a little cold but shining still on my paper, on my pen, on my beloved hands. He is happy to see me. I am happy to see me, too. The wind up here on the rock is frigid, but the beauty is stronger and my Bo tree shakes in agreement. God lives here.

The redhaired man with the glasses sits silently and chews

gum. I read haiku from *Mountain Tasting*, the book by Santoka Taneda that I bought my first vacation day in Seattle. The girl at the counter had a huge round Asian face and was surprised when I told her I came up to Washington and Oregon for Spring Break. Who leaves the warmth of south Texas to come to rain and gray skies? I do, I do, I do! And I am and I will and all of it is, just like I had hoped, and I could be here forever. The redhaired man leaves the rock, and I read poetry aloud to the ocean.

There is so much to say about this rock, with the waves slamming against it like fists, and the moss and thin grasses growing in places like patches of hair on some living being. This rock is a stalwart creature, sitting here at the boundary between land and sea, between earth and sky. The tree grows in spite of the wind, maybe grows *because* of the wind, and maybe I should as well. In spite, or because, the wind, growth—so much to learn from the silent furies of the natural world. These are fierce waters, untamed and untouched. This whole coast is untouched, it seems. There is an old, deep love here, too, like the truth of the universe, the lasting faith in What Is. I feel it moving in the marrow of my bones and under my very flesh.

I have faith in this: in humanity, in its universal youth, in its universal fallibility. I have faith in love. In hope. In generosity and kindness.

I have faith in this: Beauty. Benevolence.

I have faith in myself as creation and creator. Faith in my talents, mind, spirit, vulnerable body and lasting soul.

I have faith in this because of the blowing wind, because of my wet feet, and the single tree, and ocean sky stone beach, and breath in my lungs. When I shout, it courses through me and out into the wind, the word that is my name, that I call to the ocean and let fall like mist onto the pebbles so far below.

…oh, me. Goodness, me. Have sat and cried without tears as my feet froze and my belly burned and the sun fell through the fieriest of sunsets to the darkening waters of the Pacific. It's evening on the Oregon coast, and I've forgotten home, but I know Home, and soon I'll have to go, drive through the pines and into Portland to stay in House. Ah, day's end. I stand and look down on the shore where a small gathering of people have built a fire. They're pointing up at me. I don't think they knew I was here. I was here.

THE WOMAN

Christine Gallegos

Rising with the sun
she walks along the cliffs by the sea

Iceplant, Scotch Broom, Sweet Alyssum
shimmering puddles of color

A wind-warped tree
points an unwary stranger over the edge

Her pup is her only companion
He frolics ahead
turning back to get a nod

The ocean pumps
a strong heartbeat
smothering all other sounds

She runs, screams, whoops, beats her chest
Her pup looks back
with a puzzled cock of his black and white head

She laughs and chases him
The black hawk overhead
calls and glides with her

She is letting her hair grow long
just so the ocean wind can whip it across her face
into her mouth
so she can sputter
and spit it out

She hikes to the place where
she dares walk no further
unless she were a rock climber

She daydreams of ripping off her clothes

running down to the beach far below
into the icy water

Sometimes she sees herself
wearing a sheer Indian gauze dress
walking by the water's edge
a silhouette against the setting sun

That morning
when she gets home
her husband tells her
he read an article

Just last week
this woman
was raped
up where
she
likes to hike

That afternoon
he comes home
with a pocket-size mace sprayer
for her to carry
She puts it in her sock drawer
afraid it will attract trouble

She still walks her path
looking furtively over her shoulder
keeping her dog and spirit
reined in

She doesn't whoop
fearing it might
attract someone dangerous

No more daydreams
A woman
naked
by the sea
is vulnerable

DEEP WATERS

Jill Hammer

A synagogue of sea...
Pearls of foam adorn the wind
and cloud-spires reach into the curling air
and climb the pale blue walls,
loose-woven to hold nothing in.
Weathered by God's hands,
an ebony balcony of rock
looks out over a sanctuary of blue,
a floor of dreamy ocean, magic with the sun
bordered by the welcome of golden sand
an entrance tiled in miniature gold flecks,
warm to the toes.

Marble surf spreads out before me,
filled with the sound of a prayer
composed before the advent of voices,
and children play in the great green wings
above our gallery, rooting up the mossy cushioning,
clutching the coarse salty earth.

We women swim out to the black rock,
a dragon-shaped *amud** invented by volcanoes.
Its nooks and crannies find and hide us
like a *midrash*** deep within a text.
The water feels like painless birthing,
a mating, a making again.
The ocean drinks my dive deeply,
smooth and thirsty for me,
desiring my love.

These are living waters, holy waters,
many-layered and full of speckled life,
stretching to touch the heights at the horizon
with their frothy wave-peaks
like the pillars of song we build
in our own synagogues of wood and stone,
rushing and sparkling in the light.

amud—synagogue furniture, a lecturn for the service leader.
**midrash*—a story read between the lines of a Biblical or Talmudic
text, an interpretive parable.

THE SWAMP

Nancy Harvey

She was familiar
with that terrain:
its mud and life,
its damp smell,
the sharp high grass
and swirl of dragonfly,
water spider and mosquito,
the lavender and green
of skunk cabbage curled
along the banks.

This girl,
legs grey
with dried mud,
was an adventurer,
and the notion
of protecting this island,
this tiny nest of dry ground
in the center
of this swamp,
from all comers
filled her
until her skin burned.

That passion
for the movement of air
through experience
came at her,
traveled through her,
dimmed the sun
and flew out
through her fingertips.
She thought the birds sang

at her instruction.

There was not a moment
when she did not feel
this ecstasy.
It was a gift,
and she acknowledged it
until she had to bury it
underneath the moving water
and call it memory
or fantasy.

Now she has gone out
to find it again,
to reclaim her own land,
to mark it and name it
and call out to marauders
that it is hers
and inviolable.

In a moment of eclipse,
the sky darkens and yellows,
and she remembers her wild thoughts.
They seemed beautiful
in the swamp
but became madness
when she brought them indoors.
She will not
deny her visions any longer,
nor will she attempt
to fit them into
what she knows
as if they could be contained,
housed, domesticated.

She is afraid
someone will think

there is buried treasure here,
but there is really
nothing of value
to anyone but her.
They would not
be able to read
the signs she has pressed
into the soft dirt;
she herself is not always certain
of their meaning,
but she doesn't mind
because it is enough
to know they resonate.

The tree frogs
sound in rhythm,
and she sits among the iris,
aware that this is finite,
and while she cares about this
and about endings in general,
it is only one curious stone
among many.

It is more important
that she move her hand
along the petals
of this quiet flower,
inside its purple length,
feeling the soft sand
of pollen,
thin reed of stamen,
tracing the veins
to the brilliant yellow center.

LOST LOVE
Crystal Stone

A s I walk along the beach feeling the wind gently brushing my hair and listening to the waves of the ocean beckoning me with their thunderlike sounds, my eyes gaze at the couples occasionally laughing, embracing each other and looking passionately into one another's eyes as though the sun, the moon or the earth could not separate them. But don't they see? Don't they realize that in flash of a second everything can be gone? My eyes swell with envy as a lost tear touches my cheek.

Why do I envy them so? Because I, too, once belonged to this special group of people whose passions and desires see no ending, but only a beginning.

The sky has the warmth of a caressed bird, yet I feel cold, empty and betrayed. Who is this infinite being who decides whether we live or die?

Soon the light of day fades into darkness as the moon sprinkles bits of lighted dust across the ocean covering the beach with a cloak of desolation, darkness and cold like my soul.

Why did you have to die? You were at the peak of your life. So young, so ambitious and so loving. When I looked at what appeared to be your finality, I wondered, is this all, just a wallet and a set of keys? Is this all there is to show your existence, your life? It was as though the world had briskly pushed your life aside like it was but a speck of dust to last but only a moment.

I start to look around and see a bird flying across the edge of the sky. I hear the soft feathering of the leaves of a small tree and smell the freshness of the flowers whose odors of essence are cautiously whispering to me to come and set myself free from that from which all nature's creatures must and should arise. My heart reaches out to the bird, the flower and the soft shadows of the moon, and I realize that life must go on. But in my heart, I shall always grieve for my loved one whose hands will never be felt, whose warmth will never be enjoyed, but whose soul will go on forever in my heart.

SWIMMING BACK THROUGH LOST SEAS

Irene Keenan

D eath danced around our house. We thought he was courting my mother, but my father died instead.

I was their first child and still a child when the anger metastasized between them. I saw him slap her. I saw him batter her with words so savage that they both bled. When she cried that she had no son to defend her, I became her champion. I would charge in between them and scream at him to stop, afraid that he would turn on me, even as I dared him to, but he never did. He reserved it all for her. Me, he loved the best.

"Leave him," I said. "We'll get by."

"How can we?" she said. "It will get better."

It never did. When I was barely grown, I abandoned them. I moved as far away as I could. We spoke. We visited, I listened, we consulted, I even carried the gauntlet a few more times, but clearly I had abandoned them to their own devices.

My mother is failing now. Her skin has a clayish tint. I have a picture of her standing in a crowd of family. Old women and men look proudly at the camera, pink-skinned, white hair unruly in the morning light, some with twisted spines, some ramrod straight, some plump, all happy, surrounded by sons and daughters, grandchildren and grandnieces and nephews. We have graced them with an annual visit.

My father is one of the ruddy-cheeked, silver-haired, smiling men in the picture. Only the narrowed suspicion in his eyes betrays his inner turmoil. His smile is broad, his face unlined, while my mother gazes sorrowfully. Like a dulled ghost of a ghost, she no longer smiles.

One Saturday I went to the park with my children. On the other side of the world, my mother had gone to visit Patsy, their other daughter, my sister. Each day of her visit she'd called my father. After all, she was his wife and he had a bad heart. He was in fine spirits except for Friday, the day before she was coming home. He'd gotten a cold and why wasn't she there looking after him.

17

On Saturday my sister packed her children into the car and drove the two hours it took to get my mother home. Patsy had escaped, too, but not quite as far as I. When they arrived, the house was locked. Mom had forgotten her keys. Since no one responded to their knocking, Patsy climbed over the fence and forced open the rear door. Mom stayed out front with the grandchildren. She waited but Patsy did not appear. Finally the front door creaked open. My sister just stood there.

Mom rushed into the house. He was sitting in his chair, neatly dressed for the day, waiting for her to come home. The smell of fried bacon clung to the air. Breakfast things had been used, but not put away. His bed had been slept in. He sat in his chair with his arms flung casually out to the sides. He could have been dozing. He was still warm.

They pulled him to the floor. Crying, Patsy pressed on his chest and breathed into his mouth while my mother telephoned for help and the grandchildren watched wide-eyed. The paramedics came. It was no use, and so they left him where they found him, on the floor with my weeping sister bending over him.

Patsy called an undertaker—who took three hours to arrive. While they waited, they covered him with an orange afghan that my mother had knitted, and left him on the floor. He was too heavy to move. They took the children upstairs and all huddled in a room together until the undertaker came. No one wanted to be with the body as it lay there, inert, dominating the house for the last time.

When I got home from the park with my children, my husband met us at the door. The look on his face was so strange, my heart wrenched before he said a word.

"My mother," I cried. But I was wrong.

I arrived the next morning after a sleepless flight on a nearly empty plane. I kissed my mother on her pale, moist cheek and embraced her small shoulders. She looked utterly distraught; dangerous, dark circles threatened her eyes. She hadn't slept.

My sister and I drank coffee in the small shabby kitchen of our youth and talked quietly, aware of her every move, while she slowly wandered around, washing dishes, wiping the counter.

"I never thought he would die first," she kept repeating.

I searched for signs of relief in my mother and my sister, but I saw none. They appeared genuinely grieved. I was almost light-hearted.

The undertaker, a woman, came to arrange the burial. She explained everything in great detail so that our heads spun, and after a while we said, fine, okay, anything just so she would finish and go away. But she lumbered on. Did we want an open casket or a closed casket, did we want an individual plot or a family plot, could we get our own pallbearers, it would save us money?

"Most people plan for these times," she admonished. "It makes everything easier for all of us." When the undertaker finished, she said with a kind smile, "Your father has beautiful wavy hair."

How did she know? He'd always slicked it back. My stomach lurched. He was a corpse now. She must have looked at him. They must have washed his hair.

My sister got tranquilizers and sleeping pills prescribed for our mother who couldn't sleep. That night Patsy and I stayed in the double bed that used to be our parents.' Our mother stayed in her room that used to be my room. No one stayed in my sister's old room that our father had used.

The ordinary past stained the corners of the house where I grew up, but everything was turned around. Nothing was as it had been, nobody slept in their right bed. Nobody wanted to. I didn't feel his presence. I didn't feel his presence anywhere in the house. I waited for it. He just wasn't there anymore, but I couldn't sleep anyway.

Next day the undertaker squired us about as we chose the cemetery plot and the casket. My mother bought a cement box in which to place the casket before it was buried, even though she couldn't afford it, even though my sister and I said why? he doesn't need it, save your money. Solemnly, she told us about the sound of gravediggers shoveling dirt on cheap wooden caskets when she was a little girl in the mountains. The sound had terrified her.

At the cemetery she chose a spot on a hilltop so our feet wouldn't get muddied if it rained while we were visiting. She bought a large plot that could hold six bodies and made us promise not to bury her on top of him.

That night we distributed my mother's sleeping pills among us like girls playing doctor with candy, but we still couldn't sleep.

"Can you feel him in the house?" Patsy whispered.

I waited but I couldn't feel anything.

Rain poured the day of the funeral. I left my sister and mother at home getting ready. I went to church to meet the undertaker. In the darkened vestibule, we looked like casting call mourners in our tasteful black dresses and single strand pearls.

We stood while her assistant and her employees took the casket out of the hearse. We watched them straining as they carried the shimmering gray coffin and disappeared into church. My father had been a large man. When we were young, my mother would show us her favorite picture of him. He stood tall in his soldier's uniform in a field holding a rifle. His riveting blue eyes could dissolve the primmest virgin's reserve.

The undertaker looked at me kindly. "Do you want to see your father? He's ready for the viewing."

We walked into church together. The casket, open, surrounded by red and white carnations glowed in the dim light at the end of the long aisle ahead. Transfixed, I stared at it as we walked.

"Are you all right?" The undertaker took my arm as we promenaded down the interminable aisle toward the looming body.

It was my father. He lay there on white satin cushions with his arms by his sides. They had placed a rosary that he would never have used in the fingers of one hand. His hair was slicked back. A faint smile traced his lips.

When I was a little girl and my mother was just barely pregnant with my sister, we went to the seashore one hot Sunday in September. The beach was almost deserted so it was a perfect day. I built lumpy mounds for castles and threw sand around to my heart's content.

My father lay on the blanket nuzzling my mother's neck. His hand would stray to her breast, and she would laughingly push it away and whisper, "Baby's watching."

I was. They were so beautiful, my parents. My mother's brown velvet eyes flashed with delight as my grinning father wrestled her. He kissed her repeatedly, his mouth seeking her face, her hair, her shoulders. When I ran by screeching, he would snatch me up, throw me into the air and catch my squirming body when it flapped down again.

We sat on our blanket eating sandwiches that my mother had risen early to pack. The sun was beginning to set. My father decided that he would take me out for a swim. My mother refused to come because she did not trust the ocean. He took my hand. I looked up at him. His head thrust into the sky above his shoulders.

The cool water came and went, teasing me and tickling my legs. We waded deeper into the ocean. A wave broke in my face, I sputtered and coughed. My father picked me up. The waves couldn't even brush my toes then. We continued into the water. He lifted me in front of him and swam out deeper. In the distance I could see a dark ugly wave churning toward us. It didn't frighten me because I was with my father. I felt him stop swimming. Suddenly he turned around and started to struggle. Something was wrong. We were being forced backward. It was getting deeper. He held me against his chest. I looked over his shoulder toward the advancing wave.

"Hold your nose," he yelled. "Don't breathe."

The wave crashed over our heads. Obediently, I held my nose as we tumbled, helpless in its wake. My father gripped my arm as though he would squeeze through to the bone. The wave's rage passed over us and miraculously our heads broke through the salt water wall. My father grappled me on to his back.

"Hold tight," he said.

He started to swim toward shore. I saw a tiny figure pacing on the strand. It was my mother. When we finally reached the shore my father could barely stand. My mother had ventured in waist deep and tore me from his back.

"Are you crazy? She's just a baby. You could have both been drowned."

He collapsed in the sand gasping and stared at her. She turned her back to him and wrapping a towel around me, held me tightly. I saw him look away.

"What do you think?" the undertaker said. "Does everything look all right?"

"Oh, my God." Behind me my mother's voice cracked thick with emotion. "He's smiling. Patsy, look, he's smiling."

"He's at peace now, Mom." My sister took her arm. My mother faltered as she stepped toward her husband. One large tear pooled near the corner of a brown velvet eye rimmed in red. It swelled and bled down her gray cheek. She studied his face. What did she see? Did their life together pass through her like a shudder or a sigh? What did I know of them? Their love, their anger splashed me, washed over me like a wave until I could not breathe and swam out of the storm of their lives. When they closed the door to their room at night, they were a mystery to me.

My mother bent down and kissed him and stroked his forehead. My sister touched his hand, her face tense.

"After the viewing, before we close the casket," the undertaker instructed, "one of you must take the death blanket and, once you have said your final farewells, cover him."

"I will," I said. I was first born. He loved me best. I looked at him. He did not see me. He would never see me again, nor I him. I touched his hand. It felt cold and waxen hard, no longer flesh, but transformed by our undertaker into something else. I leaned over and kissed his brow. Suddenly I yearned for that handsome young man who so many years ago had picked me up in his strong hands and tossed me like a flower into the air and catching me, held me with such love that I never wanted him to let go. The salt of the ocean that bound us forever fell from my eye and onto his broad shoulder. I brushed it away and followed my mother and sister to sit and wait for the other mourners.

GRIEVING—HIS LIFE; SEEKING—MY LIFE

Theano Storm

That *your future gifts*
will never be known,
that *you were slain*
in the midst of blooming
(your fragrance, blown
and borne away by Winds
beyond our understanding)
still so fills me with pain
that, *Remaining* (on the Earth
you fled) has become *a daily ritual-*
of-reaching for a fruit I knew
whose sweetness had been savored,
of laboring long with aching heart and limb
to even catch a glimpse of *prize once held*,
as it hides and turns its sun-glowed cheek
to keep me searching, climbing, weeping…

Thursday, August 22nd, 1991

THE NEED TO PERMEATE MY BEING WITH THE SHARP COGNIZANCE OF YOUR MEMORY

Charlene Mary-Cath Smith

I've missed loves lost
friends moved to distant locales
even mourned longtime pets
and had secret feelings of relief
that others' dear losses
hadn't been mine But

this is monumentally different
Standing at the soon to be grassy plot
with its still barren patches
and over abundance of clover
it occurs to me
how unimportant the thought
they'll have to give it some lime
is relative
to the event
that was responsible
for my being here at all Had you left

when I was eight or ten or fourteen
instead of middle age
the missingness
could not conceivably
have been this intensely complex I want

the spot that is now your vacancy
to be filled
with the anguish the longing
for your physical body produces
the mental writhing at the thought
that that body
will never be in my presence again
the strangeness of the thought
feeling like the moment immediately
before an orgasm
yet without ever the climax I need

for it to burrow into my dermal layers
pricking and tingling
its zaps of imprint
that was is your existence Keeping

you nearer to me Keeping your having been

real

AFTERWARDS

Leonne Gould

Grief pulls down my skin
and makes me pee,
blots me with cold towels
adjusts my bones
and sucks some marrow out.

Grief blesses the small of my back,
laps at my feet
and settles me like fog.
She enlarges my pores
and spreads through my rooms
like incense.
I nuzzle into her belly
while clouds pile around me.

Grief trails behind me
like a silvery balloon
fastened to my wrist.

I rub sand into my skin,
encrust myself in metal
and poke out my arms.
I spin her down a watery beach,
my bony arms cutting into her airy back.
My teeth grow and I bite her.
I bunch her to me, cradle and pinch her.
Tears arc from my face.

I suck her down my throat
like cotton candy or gin
until she bursts
foaming like sea water
searing my gums.
Then I spit her out.

I become a giant
with breasts like battlements.
I go home, bathe and oil myself.
Then I dress in all my colors,
and wait.

BEDBUGS

Catharine Clark-Sayles

I thought of you today when I saw the iris bloom
And recalled the muddy knobbed roots
You daughter brought last year
Because you loved them best

I thought of your tiny birdlike voice
From somewhere in that enormous bed
Walnut, carved with flowers and beasts
With its heaps of downy quilts

Ninety was a good age; ninety-five beyond all hope
But it seemed a shame for you to die
When your daughter gave such care
As if by force of will she could keep you here

When you could not walk, her back became your strength
her legs became your limbs
Hour on patient hour she would spoon each sip
Into your mouth rigid with its palsied shake

When I would tiptoe in you were so still
I could not believe such tiny bones could hold
Anything so coarse as life
But your daughter would say "Sleep tight"

And in that great carved bed where you were born
Your tiny voice would chirp "Don't let the bedbugs bite"
When your daughter asks again, as she will
If there was something she could have changed

If anything was left undone
I will remind her of her gift:
To let you die gently, safe, and warm
In the bed where you were born.

CRAZED COOKIES

Renee Norman

my mother
>expecting death
baked sesame twist cookies all morning
waiting for the phone to ring
answering machine turned to off

my mother
>recognizing death
in the hospital waiting room
went home and
feeling nervous
worked in her blue kitchen
where she knew the phone would ring
as surely as the tulips lost
their petals to the wind
every springtime

my mother
>foreshadowing death
filled her freezer with those cookies
rows of twisted dough corpses
packed in shoebox coffins
defrosting them
only two days later

my mother
>no stranger, she said, to death
served those cookies
cleared the plates that held them
vacuumed sesame seeds from
rug corners
and said,
prepare yourself
but don't let it make you crazy

PETAL CHILD

Cora Greenhill

There is no way
there is no right way
we have not been taught
any way of being
with this
have no hammock of belief
to lie back in
no sustaining truth
to feed us in this wilderness of loss.

We have no rites passed down
for your passing on
can only listen to what our hearts invent
allow all our hearts to invent
from their love and grief
each in our own way
for all of us

But after the days of womanly waiting
the still ache of unknowing
the suspension of active life
in the blank ignorance of daylight
while inside life and death
held silent conference

and after my night of untimely labour
when the body decreed
I must use my ancient knowledge
of birth breathing
against the painful spasms

that leave no room for doubt,

when I have no choice but to co-operate
in freeing you
from the greedy embrace of my flesh
our flesh
life's playtime from eternity

when you, the closest
of all lives to me
are already leaving me
before we've met
gone on ahead
leaving me
the uninvited guest

you linger awhile in the ether
dandled in my trance of love
dancing with your company of souls
one new petal brighter than the many
shining your good bye
waving God by me
to comfort me
you comfort me
oh my daughter.

CHILI BEANS

Nancy McGovern

Didn't know who you were at first
Even awoke
To see the time
As from a nightmare
Chilled
Getting my attention
I retraced it all
Seemed to be my Grandma
In the blur of sleepy recall

Broken glasses caved in
On flattened and cracked brown eyes
But Grandma had blue eyes

I had come to a house
To eat chili beans
You in the other room
I approached with anxiety
To find
A shrunken body
Wrapped in a black baby blanket
Picking you up
I carried you through the house
Feeling the awesome smallness
Of your form
On my arm.

Near the time
Returning
You retreated sinking
Inward
Going away
And following
I put my head to your cheek
Hearing from deep in your sleep
Far away,

Good-bye Nancy
I hope you enjoy your chili beans

Today
Kept thinking of who had brown eyes
Glasses
Old person the way
The old-lady black spinster boots
Had hung from the blanket
Predominantly large

Then I remembered
How you had aged
While the disease drained you that year

Insignificant conversations we had had
Before AIDS started in on you
About how to survive
When there was never enough money,
Beans I said
Chili beans are great

It's been five summers
Since that night in the hospital
Haven't been able
To write a word about any of it
Speak anymore of it
A rock
Blocking a passage
In my heart
Anger
Guilt
Oppression
No one could do anything
To make
Anything better

Doctors who bandaged
This and that infection
Over and over

Their prejudiced attitudes
Barely concealed
Behind professionalism
Their muted frustration
Couldn't just cut something out
And whop it with antibiotics or chemotherapy
Or turn to a page
In a medical volume

There was no help
And in the end
No chance to say good-bye
The
Beep
Beep
Beep
Stopped
Flattening the green line of the ticker-taker
To silence

I asked for the time, 2:13 a.m.
Five summers ago

In the dream last night
I asked for the time, 2:16 a.m.

Hard to remove a blockage,
I should have known who you were
But I wanted
To forget your suffering
And mine as well
In our friendship
I have felt like a failure
That I couldn't lift you
Somehow
A little
From your descent

Thank you for saying good-bye

CATCHING SWALLOWS

Vanessa Gang

Swallowing
to catch her breath
between sobs,
my daughter remembered
being four. In a rush
or words rising
like bubbles
from the bottom,
she was giving names
to images darting
like swallows.
Seizing them,
one by one, she was
catching swallows
by the tail:

Was it night? she asked.
I remember dark and the men.
Was there an ambulance?
I remember waiting.
You said I could
say Good-bye. Waiting,
I wrote "I love you
Daddy" on the blackboard.
I couldn't talk to you, Mommy.
You were with the men.
Did the men take him?
I didn't hear him leave.
You said I could say Good-bye,
but you forgot, and he...,
nobody told me, Mommy,
he had already died.

This solitary promise
unkept, between us
every word since.
Words buried
between us. Not him.
My words...
Buried between us:
The large acid truth of Good-bye.

EXCERPT FROM A LETTER TO A FRIEND
Lee Anne Grundish

—layers of a Life we now must try to learn to live, again—
Again. The matriarchs who go
on dying. Borne out of sight, but not away, and cast us to
this intimate storm, where nothing comforts and nothing will rest
and nothing keeps that death at bay. And nothing leaves the pain
alone. Wild myth, her.   Infinite
shelter. Infinite warm. Gone. Luminescent, she will be
omnipresent. *She* to some intimate power. And we
can only honor   the line of women from whom

                    we come,

                      stepping forward
with love for one and one another and a certain
emotional protest of memory that keeps
one death   away.   (and everywhere i went
                    the blessings she had
                    sent had gone before
                      me where i'd go
and never knew but now
i know) It may be all that we can do.   I wonder
if they dance up there together—celebration!   though
i suppose i might envision something much
more somber.   And sincere, devoid of
touch. (or pain. or fear.)   Constant vigilance
and review. Like life. But I
can dance right here, tonight.
With you.

And I have made it through. And so
must you. And so
will
you.

ANGELS

Priscilla Rhoades

My bed feels empty without you in it, without
your soft breathing beside me, your sweet presence
in the night. Last night I slept lightly

sweating between waking and dreaming, and I prayed
for a cool, green place. In the quiet I saw eagles
and angels and dogs running in a pack.

Sharna saw an angel standing in the doorway
to the church and heard another
whisper her name. You told me the story.

And when I was seven I felt an angel
brush my shoulder, one night, by the dark tree
in the backyard. On a branch a rat hesitated,
a black silhouette in the moonlight, and someone
whispered under the wind. I wasn't afraid.

The cancer is a small thing, it is a coin
someone gave you a long time ago. You took it
without thinking, cupping it in your hand
the way a child tries to keep water
or a secret. You have carried it with you
all these years, a token of that other journey.
You don't need it here.

There is a landscape beyond this moment
and a greener country inside your eyes;
there is a place that is holy
and a promise that needs to be broken.

There are lovers and eagles and dogs
running in a pack, and there are angels
around us and angels all around

and there are, most assuredly,
angels all around.

WAITING (for Gloria)

Judy Powell

[1]
A woman stands in the center of a field

A yellow sun with white-hot center,
a crayon blue sky,
one cloud that floats, indifferent,
thin as a feather
on the hot wind:
a woman stands in the center of the field.

Her feet are rooted in the cracked earth.
Locusts feed and sing in the tall grass.
Butterflies bend on wild flowers,
white and yellow wings,
white and yellow petals.

The woman holds a jar spun from the earth,
rough, circle upon circle;
a jar so large arms cannot reach,
fingers do not touch;
a jar born of the night,
no stars, moon lost.

The woman and the jar are one,
weight balanced to weight.
It is a dream.
No other eyes, no other arms.

There are secrets in the jar:
flutes and laughter,
islands lost in mist,
nightwind from the mountains,
animals, evergreens, snow.

Somewhere the seasons change.
It is a long journey out.
The woman rocks the jar like a child.
She sways and waits for the moon to come,
new, delicate,
a white porcelain moon
rising in the east.

[2]
Twenty years ago on this day they were married.

Today he is buried in the little cemetery

on the hill on Big Buck Road.

She is sitting on a large flat rock
in the middle of a stream in the Tetons
in a place they have been together many times.

Today they are not together.

She has made this journey alone.
Walked twelve miles up into the mountains
with fifty pounds on her back.
She has come to know she is alone.
To embrace the nightmare.

She sits very still.
And she will sit this way for hours.
She is empty. Open.
She is listening to the breathing
of the mountain,
the water rushing,
the wind.
There is nothing left of her
but this listening.
This waiting.

She meant to go with him.
Thought, at first, she would go before him.
Prepared, even longed, for her own death.
When was it decided otherwise?
Empty out the questions.
There is only this:

She did not go with him.
She has lived his death as her own.
Peeled away her self like dead skin.
Red, raw, exposed,
she has chosen these mountains,
this rock,
this moment.

She has chosen life.
This breathing in and out.
Within this choice,
within this rhythm,
in and out,
she will begin to heal.

It is a prayer for her.

A WIDOW'S MOURNING FANTASIES

Margaret Hehman-Smith

Yearning for You

My feeling of loss is an ancient ache, an emptiness from past knowledge, past loves, swimming through ageless rivers…

Your face, ethereal, vaporous, looks five times into mine, passing through me the fifth time. Your tongue falls on air and returns to warmth. We repeat each other, ascending and descending. Distant noises echo like sounds of breathing. Many hands touch, many legs flail, many bodies ecstatically mingle.

Now, with the morninglight pressing on, love surges in my heart and hastens the sunrise. Finches and doves proclaim their existence.

Ancient Aerosols

This morning, the trees were in my room with their afterrain fragrances. The cool breeze whistled through my mouth. I remember when you said you were going to sell your cure "guaranteed to fill the hole in the pit of the stomach." This morning I needed a dose of it but the rain forest helped. You sat monkey-like in the highest tree, smiling and pointing your finger at me.

The rain started up again and then I could hear a trickle of a stream. I was on the mountain looking down a deep canyon. You had climbed down the tree and took my hand. We started walking, kicking up the dust on the crest. "Are you hungry?" you asked.

Tonight, you will unfold the layers and the covers from muscle, bone, mind and spirit. You will tease old hurts from determined blocks.

Scenes will spurt from ancient aerosols, leaving a trail of skeletal feet whose footprints are ready to return to earth as fertilizer for seeds of the future. Past seeds have sprouted and we are harvesting them now.

And if the days don't make sense, I'll go where you wanted to walk, along the edge where birds flew to see us. You needed love and I decided loving you was the most important dream. Back then we could see the sky.

Joy of the Spirit

I feel it, like a breeze, soft across my body, spreading, like islands of refreshment that tingles stale air.

Joy has no sight but your joy touches me with degrees of intensity.

My life continues on like blood. Moving blood covers more miles through veins and arteries than all the rivers of the world.

Days lengthen, autumn leaves turning into thoughts of you. Once again, our mouths repeat the same fired words. I see your eyes shining through ages of hazes connecting with my vision.

You hold out your arms enfolding my mind and body. Oh, joy!

WIDOW
Tova Green

This poem was written after a visit with the widow of a well-loved writer.

I live two lives.
In Dubrovnik I am
still his widow.
I paint at night,
in the dark, the island,
standing only a few meters
from the kitchen
where he died.
A shell exploded.
He was killed,
I survived. His blood
stains the stone floor still.
We were together
eleven years. We met
at a friend's wedding,
fell in love instantly.
He, a Serb, was killed
by a Serbian shell.

In Belgrade I am
Yelena, the painter.
I have friends there,
sisters. After he died
I went to Belgrade to tell
of the shelling of Dubrovnik.
They did not know.
My friends in Belgrade
did not want war.

In Dubrovnik
people do not understand me.
How can I not hate, they ask.

Yet I too am a Serb.
In Dubrovnik
I am an island.
I wear dark colors.
Every day I swim
in the sea, drink
black coffee in my
favorite cafes, talk
with friends. At night
I paint my island.

After he died
friends opened
a bank account for me.
Someone left twelve eggs
on my doorstep. An egg
is precious in war.

I used to make collages.
My last collage I named
"widow," finished two days
before he died. He
did not like it. We
never discussed it, or
the dreams of war I had before
the shelling began.

I grew up after he died. Now
I know what is
important, what is not. Who is
my friend, who is not.

Showing you the photo album,
his books, the holes
in the walls, I feel heavy. Yet
I want to tell you
everything. Then I am not
an island.

MEMORY'S BURDEN

Fran Peavy

It's hard to come back to my home
 my mind returns to the refugees' faces
 in a moment the memory takes over with the stories of
  their difficult lives
  of their dignity in the face of loss
   of the deep questions about trust and human
   nature.
   What hunger does this war feed?
Back in America and its fascination with the sordid details of
 murder and sex
 The questions posed by Eastern Europe pull at me.
  What institutions can stop the fighting?
   Driving down the road I do not see bombed out
    houses
    Troops at checkpoints
     village people walking along with a slump in
     their shoulders.
Home sadness—that's what I saw
 that's what touched me.
  Forced to leave their homes each fragile human had
   moved to the horizon,
   many reported that when they looked back they saw
    only a pile of stones
    where their homes, their farms, their lives had
    been.
     Where their ancestors had tilled the soil for
     generations.
  "I remember my cow," one old man remembers.
  "I remember" he speaks looking out through the walls
   of the refugee camp
   out past the city which now holds his body
   he looks beyond fertile hills of the land around him
    remembering his own fertile hills in Slovenia or
    Bosnia.

His memory penetrates the still wet national borders
painted with the blood of homes and of the
young who went to fight
because someone said it was the thing to do.
The not-really-the-enemy army prevents him from returning to
find his cow.
"There is no home there for me now. As I left I saw it
burning."
So the man steps to the center of the circle and sings of his cow
tears dropping from his hollow sun withered cheeks.
He knows nothing else is still standing.
The old man remembers his cow.
His eyes scream such piercing questions
"How did this happen to us?"
Broken hearted, he is a refugee.
Broken hearted, I remember him. When it gets cold
I will remember there is no heat in his room.

SWALLOWS OF WAR
Rhiannon

Does the war change the song of the birds?
The swallows careening through the air
in the old walled city of Dubrovnik.
Crying and calling around the statue of the W.W.II partisan
in the square at Novi Sad.

Do they sing a different song
now that they've seen war
heard cannons
felt bombs drop?

Did the smoke clog their lungs and stop their song?
Did they hide until it was over?
Did birds die in battle?
Caught in the middle.
Innocents of war.

I ask this question over and over.
Is it because I can't bear to ask the other questions stuck inside me?
Questions that come from the eyes of humans.
Human refugees who can't go home—don't have a home—lost
            everything
They sit with me singing call and response.
For a moment their eyes light up.
When we sing songs—theirs and mine—there is so much crying.
Deep sorrow comes over the room and in another moment we are
            laughing
about the lake of tears inside and how we must laugh anyway.

These memories
Avramovic´ Arsova
come like a dull ache.
His 16 year old body full of boot marks

full of loss
empty.
But he sings and holds my hands,
puts his arms around my neck for a photo
says I remind him of his mother.
Old women in black from Slavonia
some old men, not many.
They sing of the rolling hills, milk cows, sunflower fields.
They lost everything—again.

All these memories pile up
and I still don't know if the song of the birds changes.
If everything is so much loss, so much terror,
so much sadness and rage,
how can the birds not be affected?
How can it be their ancient song would just stay the same?

Crying and calling
Flying in packs, in flocks, in circles,
turning just at the last moment,
turning together
flying out free
returning to the fold.

Sing. Sing on. Sing on endlessly.
NO MORE WAR!

FINAL POEM FOR DALIBOR
Vesna Dye

Suddenly, the game of seagulls is over
at sunset, on your island where chiming of the old clock
still outcries the shrapnels

You talked to me about their wings
spread above your cove:
white flags of peace in the twilight of our hopes

You said: seagulls will survive the crumbling rocks
they will shriek louder than the sea—
the tombstone for nameless bodies
sun is the only witness of atrocities
numb priest who forgives everyone
even those that cut throats instead of bread

And you believed
they would at least spare the seagulls
a bird belongs to the sky
and a man always returns to the earth

But look—a bird is hit in the eye
the sea turns crimson from its tears
and your heart becomes silent before the onset of the tides

WHAT THEY KNEW

Gloria Dyc

What are we looking for
when we dig, measure and map?
We find mammoths sealed in ice
cloth and seeds mummified in the desert
We unearth cities and the bones of humans
marvel at the age of the planet
and our short and fragile tenure
In the beginning there was bare rock and sea
We watch the Colorado wear its way
into the rock of six million years
We map the retreat of the seas
the drift of the continents
We dig and find pots arrowheads jewelry
Egyptian tombs Greek theatres Pueblo cities
And we ask: What did they know?

Babylon is entombed in the desert of Iraq
under five thousand years of sand
The city was organized by streets
which intersected at right angles
Algebra was in use at that time
Gold, silver and copper were used in trade
They perfected their technology
in seige machinery and war chariots
They knew a class system, royalty
slaves and military rule
They were the first to capture and deport Jews
Conquest and insurrection were common
The bricks from the ancient royal houses
were pilfered and used elsewhere finally
Once after the eclipse of the sun
there was anarchy

The sky over Baghdad is lit tonight
in shades of white and green and red

the light show of a military so advanced
we shudder at our capacity to destroy
and worry more about the pyramids
birthplaces of the prophets
stone tablets city of Babylon
than the wailing of women
or the starvation of children
And we know one day it may not be some "other"
but we ourselves who will be uncovered
cast in ash and molten rubble
like the man found in the shadow of Vesuvius
arms outstretched, one hand protecting his mouth
one last gasp of precious air

TO THE GIRL WHO LOOKS PERFECTLY WHITE OUTSIDE BUT IS PERFECTLY HALF MIDDLE EASTERN WITHIN

Gwendolyn Raver

When she unhooks the bra
or slides down ripped pants
She is revealed.

In the most private places
East overran West
The Night beat the Sun
and she is revealed.

Arab-esque, not a hundred percent
She has not fully arrived.
The terrorist spying around corners
or the wisps of hair fallen from veil
Her heritage sneaks back.

It whispers, it sighs
It never announces itself.
It is the whiff of hummos
and roasting coffee
The clink of metal on metal
in the dance
and her grandmother's ululation,
with wrinkled hands proudly clapped.

In her private parts
and private thoughts
the ancestors survive.
But only there,
under wraps,
they whisper.

THINGS THAT MATTER
Alethea Eason

I t could be your last chance," Carol said. "First and last."

Terri's arms crossed against her chest. Colder than she had been all day, she had just slipped on her wool sweater, but it was her friend's words, not the chill caused by the setting sun, that made her hug herself.

She'd put her hair in a clip that morning, but most of it now fell in waves to her shoulders, fading from shades of brown to silver. As a runner she stayed thin, but in the last week she sensed the first fullness in her body.

She had tried living with the man who fathered what was inside of her. After a month they were fighting. Like the men before, but in the past, thinking she should never be a mother, she had always been careful. She thought she had been again. That's what she told Mitch before he screamed at her. She promised herself she would make a decision while camped on this trip.

Vulture-sized mosquitoes held the two women captive in the cab of the truck on a deserty slope above the town of Big Pine. Terri listened to the wind talk as it beat against the door. She closed her eyes and could almost hear the words. She hoped they would tell her how to make up her mind, but a Toyota pick-up was too prosaic a place for divination. The wind kept mumbling.

The Sierras stretched in a line on the other side of the valley, looking hungry here in the lower part of the range with jagged tops like teeth raked across the darkening sky. The snow hung low on the mountain sides, sagebrush and snow deep violet now. Hues of purple reflecting off the mountains had been shadowing across the valley for the last half hour.

Carol leaned over the seat and kissed Terri who allowed the kiss for one moment and then pushed her back.

"But you've thought about it?" Carol's hand rested on Terri's arm. She looked at her intently trying to get a sense of what she really felt.

"It would be a good way to ruin a friendship." Terri took Carol's hand, patting it between her own. Feeling awkward, she said, "I'm the one uncomfortable here, aren't I?"

Months before, drinking wine, papers sprawled around them on her sofa, Carol had hinted. Terri changed the subject and looked at a math page with more care than necessary, but Carol was right. She had thought about it, and it scared her silly.

Carol looked like a school teacher with short blonde hair that was rarely out of place. She was divorced and raised her two daughters in a house that was always immaculately clean. Terri teased her because she ironed everything, even her t-shirts and jeans.

Three years before, Carol had met a woman who had come to town to take care of her dying sister. The six months she was there had changed Carol's life. Terri knew; no one else did.

It surprised Carol when Terri got the job teaching first grade. She was at times frenetic, and it was evident she disliked structure, something the school prided itself on. Her classroom mirrored the messiness of her truck. It was rarely quiet, but from the very beginning, the children thrived in her care.

Terri's quirkiness appealed to Carol. The two soon discovered there was another person in town who read more than the best sellers on the rack at the grocery store. Carol wondered how she had made it five years with no one to talk to about things that mattered.

One afternoon Carol came into Terri's room to say good bye but began watching the rat that had just delivered. Seven pink lumps hung from her as she walked across the cage. Carol noticed the eighth lump in the corner.

"I think one of them died," she said.

Terri scrubbed tempera from the sink. "Born dead. I haven't been able to touch it."

Carol reached in and took it out. "Poor thing," she said, and then made a face. "What do I do with it?"

"In the trash can, I guess." Terri dried her hands. "Thanks. I couldn't watch when the babies were being born."

Carol sat on a desk. "That surprises me."

Terri brushed her hand through her hair nervously. "I can't stand helplessness."

Carol needed to get dinner going, but she stayed. The two talked for a long time about the things they were both hiding.

On Back to School Night, a year after they began working together, they lined up in the cafeteria with the rest of the staff.

The principal introduced Carol as the "perky" teacher.

She whispered to Terri, "I hate it when people call me that."

Terri whispered back, behind her hand, "Like a fucking cheerleader." The principal called Terri's name and she smiled at the parents, and then, in a moment of revelation, whispered again, "You were a cheerleader, weren't you?"

"What if I was?"

"I'm just jealous. I was never popular."

The PTA president began to talk. Carol spoke as softly as she could, "People expected it of me."

"I was always too serious." The teacher standing next to Terri shushed her, but she had one more thing to whisper in Carol's ear. "Do you think we would have been friends then?"

Carol shrugged her shoulders. "Who's to say?"

Carol leaned back against the car seat. They sat in silence. Terri peered through the windshield. How shallow her breath was. She hadn't spoken to Mitch in a week. She was yelling, "Get the hell out of my life!" to his back the last time she saw him, drained of dignity from threatening him with doing harm to herself if he left. She hadn't felt much since, not wanting to bring that needy creature back to life.

"I inherited my mother's way with people who come too close. I can't imagine it would be any different with you."

She got out of the truck before Carol responded. A bat swooped by her head. She hurried to unroll the foam mattress and her sleeping bag.

There was one large rock. She went behind it to pee. They had been here for two hours without anyone driving by, but as soon as she squatted, headlights hit the rock. She waited for the car to pass, wondering who would be driving toward the emptiness of Nevada. When it was gone she stood and watched the taillights zigzag up the road, two red eyes in the night. She watched until they winked and were gone, then leaned against the rock, her fingers spread on its rough surface for support, trying to mask her panic in the darkness. Carol was her friend, that was what mattered more than anything. She needed a friend now.

Ten minutes later, warm in her bag, she noticed the wind had stopped its jabbering. Carol sat up, pulling her bag around her head. "There's just one car going down 395," she said. Without looking at Terri, she asked, "Do you at least feel closer to deciding?"

"I was just thinking of wanting to hit Ethan last year. He was always hanging on me."

"We all feel that way at times. It doesn't mean you'll beat your child."

"I grabbed him once like this," Terri sat up and squeezed Carol's shoulder. "But I was squeezing really hard, and I sat him down in his chair. I could tell by his face I was hurting him. I kept thinking, oh my God, what if I leave marks, but I kept squeezing."

"You love children, Terri."

"But what if I'm a Nazi mama when no one is looking?"

"You're not your mother."

Terri didn't say anything but took her glasses off and lay down again. The stars disappeared, but the moon rose like an odd-shaped mandala of light, cold as the desert. She thought of the animals out on the sand, hunting, crouching, scurrying to hiding places. Mothers giving birth to their young. She thought of her mother's hands around her throat, shaking her. She put her hands on her belly and dug her nails into her skin.

"I'd be there to help you," Carol said, adjusting her bag and lying down too. "No matter what between us. We could take care of the baby together."

"You love them, don't you?"

"Mmmm," Carol said sleepily. "So would you."

The next morning the frost on the ground crunched under their shoes. Their lungs stung from the cold air.

"Hiking at 9,000 feet at seven in the morning? This is a vacation?" Carol asked.

"Keep going. It's worth it."

They were surrounded by the oldest living things in the world. Bristle Cone pines, gnarled and squat, bearing life in the most essential way. One branch or two on each tree twisting in khaki green. The rest gray and dying, warped like a forest of Rumplestiltzkins.

They reached the crest of the trail. A small sign proclaimed it a photographers' point.

"I'd like to rip that sign up," Carol said. "I hate being told what to think, especially in a place like this. There is no wilderness any more, Terri. No places that are truly wild."

The wind blew hard now that the sun was up. Terri felt her hair tangling.

She said simply, "Look at the view."

They stood for a long time. The wind at their hearts, eyes following the path of ancient life, the earth, the oldest things, strata of rock layered and folded. They stood so still a pika climbed on a rock and rested with them. Terri looked at him. He ran to a shadow.

Carol put her hand on Terri's back. Terri turned and faced her, their arms encircling each other. It was surprising to hold another woman, the smallness of it, the bones fine and different from the bulk of men, the softness of the cheeks and the lips. Carol placed her hand on Terri's breast.

She took it away.

"I feel like I'm fifteen in the school parking lot after the basketball game."

"Being good?"

"Perhaps."

Terri felt a hunger dense as granite, something hard like a stone that would not feed her. In the middle of the hunger the panic clawed. She ran from Carol, down the path, and by the time she got to the truck she was shaking. When Carol reached the parking lot Terri's fingers were numb from gripping the steering wheel.

"Turn the heater on," Carol said, climbing into the truck. Not waiting for Terri, she snapped it on. "I didn't mean to upset you."

Terri turned on the ignition and drove down the mountain in silence.

Carol took a sip from the bottle of water they carried and handed it to her. The water was still cold from sitting out all night.

Terri stopped and looked at a map. "North to Reno or south to Death Valley?"

"It's your call," Carol said.

Terri chose a road at random and hoped she was driving somewhere.

CO-DEPENDENT

Lian Njo

Uninvited I join him
We lean back to get comfortable
In plush seats of unconsciousness
I squeeze myself into his seat
Press my face against his tinted window
Wait for wheels to slide
Travel miles
Over rails of solid steel.

The whistle
Raw signal of departure
Was only make believe
Beneath me wheels grind
Miles never traveled
Into rails of solid steel
While outside his tinted window
A world moves on.

LEAVING HIM AND STARTING OVER
maryellen

Six years ago, I made the most important decision of my life, a decision which has altered the course of my existence. I left my abusive husband for the last time; I filed for divorce. Now, I have nearly completed a professional graduate degree, and will soon have the opportunity to work in an area where I can help others.

My decision and what followed have not been without cost. *It has cost me a great deal*—psychologically, emotionally, and spiritually—but I think I have definitely come a long way from those days when I cowered in the corner waiting for my ex-husband to find me and assault me, choke me until I passed out, or viciously kick and punch me.

Why has it been so difficult? Well, it was very hard to leave my abusive husband, because I had become very helpless about having any control over my life, and because I feared that he would kill me. I found later, when we were in court, that the judges knew about "the battered woman syndrome" and were unforgiving of such victimization.

In addition, I had tried to leave the marriage a number of times, but I always returned—at first, because he promised the abuse would stop, and later, because he threatened that I would never see the children again if I left.

I had to get to a point where there was no choice before I left. I had thought that I could try to please him, that I could prove to him that I loved him, that he would once again show the affection and attention he had pretended to show when we were going out together. This didn't happen because I was doing all the trying, and he was not trying at all. I was so severely depressed that I was hanging on to life by a thread. My ex-husband continually demeaned me in front of the children, always contradicted any decision for which they came to me, and I felt they might be happier without me, without the confusion. The real risk was that either I would have killed myself, or my ex-husband would have killed me.

Fortunately, I realized that I needed to get help with the depression. I went to the ER of a nearby general hospital and was easily admitted to the psychiatric unit. After a couple of weeks, my doctor said to me, "We don't want to break up your family, but if you decide to leave, we will help you." We planned a weekend at home for me, but my ex-husband forced it to be cancelled, when he demanded that I make some kind of written statement that I would never be hospitalized again—another no-win situation in a no-win marriage.

Shortly after this, still in the hospital, I had what some people call my "emotional divorce"—that moment when I realized that the marriage was over, that he didn't love me, that there was no hope of a change. So I filed for divorce, the hospital personnel were able to find an attorney, who worked with me for the next two years, after I left the hospital and started living in a rented room in a large home.

The divorce proceedings took two years; we have no-fault divorce in my state, so a divorce was inevitable, but my ex-husband, acting *pro se*, tried everything to make this the most horrible process. When the divorce was final, we received joint legal custody, but because I was still in intensive therapy and unable to work full time, the children resided with their father. My visitation rights were liberal, but something happened which I had never even considered.

My ex-husband convinced the children that I had abandoned them—he returned my letters to them, and wouldn't tell them where I was, wouldn't let them visit me regularly. It has now been almost three years since I have visited with my kids because they say they do not want to have anything to do with me.

If you knew me, and if you had met my ex-husband, you would understand that what has happened to me is completely unfair. The abuser continues to abuse; the difference is that I no longer will be victim.

So it has been hard, VERY hard, but now I believe in myself, I believe in tomorrow, and I just have to live with the pain that can't be taken away.

AIN'T I A WOMAN! AIN'T I A WOMAN!

Monica Gunning

Strong black woman, like a tree
Sends down deep roots.
Harriet Tubman saw all her children
Sold into slavery, one by one,
Never, never to see their pleading eyes again.
The grief in her heart she bore alone;
None but God knew her sorrow's deep pain;
Yet she exclaimed, while tears cooled her face,
"Ain't I a woman! Ain't I a woman!"

Strong black woman today,
Accepts her role;
Strokes her child's head, says, "Love ya honey!"
Tells another, "Mi chile, stay in school
To have a better life than your Mom
Who struggles to pay rent, and buy bread."
Like a willow when harsh winds blow,
Strong black woman cries out, "I won't break,
Ain't I a woman! Ain't I a woman!"

AN EPIC TALE

B.J. Swan

September 9
The Poetry class at UCSD was overbooked. Aspiring crashers
were given the following option:
*"Have some work on my desk at 9 tomorrow morning, and
we'll see!"*

September 10, 8:45 a.m.
> Dear Professor Fussell:
> I feel uncomfortable doing this,
> asking for favors, I mean.
> At least I can promise nothing maudlin
> no begging scene
> instead I'll gently tell my tale
> hoping it won't bend your ear
> of how my present plight evolved
> and why, after all, I'm here...
>
> *I.*
> Once upon a time, not long after they
> invented the wheel
> fresh from winning The Real War
> the way all ex-Marines feel
> took my G.I. Bill and *really meant*
> to go to school
> then Pan Am beckoned, glamour won
> I stayed an uneducated fool
> so true, the old saw
> time does fly when you're having fun
> just a vain airborne cutie pie
> hostessing on the London run...
>
> *II.*
> Spaced out in so many ways
> feet hardly ever touched the ground
> suddenly found myself married and pregnant
> or was it the other way around?
> (Trust me, he says.
> You know the sort.

Those were the days
nice girls did not abort.)
But no regrets
that bouncing baby boy
was a living cliche
a bundle of joy
in fact, the formula worked so well
thought we'd have another
must've got it right
Pete now had a baby brother…

III.
Ah, Dad was a charmer
my love so true
life filled with laughs
till the bills came due
moved north to south
keeping one jump ahead
seemed we like to never
got out of the red
memories of journeys
unforgettable
uncomfortable, but not
regrettable
working here and there
along the way
always looking
for a better day…

IV.
Oh, blessed hindsight
with 20/20 vision
I'd take that past again
in instant decision
we lived and loved
in Washington State
broke and cold
cooked over a grate
in a tarpaper shack
and not much more
had to suck in your gut

to open the door
only 3 windows
each holding a sight so clear
of the Cascades, the Olympics,
and Mount Rainier...

V.

Onward moves the caravan
Niagara Falls in summer
is heavenly
winter's a bummer
hell freezes over
so do the Falls
icy northern breezes
once more pierce the walls
"Take me
where that sun do shine,
and the magnolias blossom
all the time,"
I cried. My pleas bore fruit...

VI.

On the road again
south to Florida
stopping now and then
to fix a flat
change a diaper
buy some gas
pay the piper
hit that sunshine
and balmy breeze
didn't stop
till we hit the Keys
that old baby-making recipe
got resurrected
here's a girl, then a boy
this time we really had it perfected
all huddled together
through Hurricane Donna
survived in good health
though the house was a goner...

VII.
Not so lucky
one sad day
Tom and the boys
sailed away
the boat turned over
in a sudden squall
pop got cramps and
couldn't swim at all
Scotty tried
to save his dad
the strain was too much
for the lad
Pete swam it in
a nine mile haul
they never found those two at all...

VIII.
Stop!
This is not a call for pity.
Listen,
life rolls on in the big city
and in the Keys as well
mom was able
to letter boats
wait on table
design clothes
make rich ladies' dresses
write stories for Miami's Herald
Stop the Presses!
Scout mother to the world
from Cubs to Explorers
Brownies, Cheerleaders,
pajama party horrors...

IX.
While working as a travel agent
(yep, that, too)
thought I'd check out
some place new
San Diego

grabbed my heart
a voice whispered
"'tis time to part
from skeeters, mildew,
and constant sweat,
before these bones
take a permanent set"
sold the house I built myself
tucked the memories on a shelf
swapped a Ford
that barely ran
for an ugly yellow van
filled it full
of bare essentials
left behind
inconsequentials
even bleached my graying hair
(a waste of time; roots are still there)
trucked on out
to this laid back land
far out, man
like, I mean, it's grand...

X.
Stayed legit
in a nine-to-five
till all my bees
had left the hive
now old granny's
free at last
runs 10Ks
(but not too fast)
backpacks weekends with the Sierra Club
catch me nights at the Rathskeller serving grub
full time Junior at UCSD
now who'd 'a thunk it?
but here's my hardest test yet
please, Professor, don't let me flunk it.

Sincerely, June

P.S. Made the class.

PASSING TIME
Brooke Silverbrand

She sits on the old wooden rocking chair
Staring out the ancient window
Not a motion made
Not a word said
Not a sound to be heard.

What is she thinking?
What does she know?
Does she know where she is?
Does she know who she is?
Does she know why I'm here?

I wish she would talk.
I wish she would walk or move.
I wish that she would hug me or kiss me
and tell me she loves me.

Do I hug her?
Do I speak to her?
Should I kiss her?
Is it O.K. to be nervous?
Is it O.K. to cry?

As it starts to get darker the nurse comes in and gets her back
on her bed. Then I leave, with tears streaming down my
cheeks.

GRANDMA

Juliana Neely

Poor, poor Grandma.
Slow-moving,
Fragile.
With ankles so thin I think I could wrap my fingers
around them twice.
Suddenly I'm as tall as she and ten times as strong.

Now there's a new home in a hall of doors,
A small room but enough for her.
We feel like robbers going through her things,
Forcing her to decide what to keep or give.
Packing up her old life,
Setting up her future.
Keeping her dreams safe within our hearts.

FAMILY DIVISIONS

Sally Reeves

I wake up this morning and it is pouring with rain; I can hear it banging on the roof and skylight windows. I wonder if my mother has woken up yet, in her familiar bed in her new strange room. I think about whether she knows where she is at the moment of waking and how she feels about it when she realises. I awake with my stomach churning and remember exam days, interviews and visits to the dentist.

She has not been able to express any feelings or worries, only practical concerns like how the bath times are organised and whether she can take her breakfast back to her room in the mornings. I wonder how she felt when my sister and her husband drove away yesterday, leaving her to her new old life. I imagine it as a little like I felt when my parents drove out of the school gate or grew smaller and smaller, still waving as Southampton station receded.

Today we are going to sort out her possessions, the day of the division of the spoils. I had always imagined she would be dead when we had to do this, but she isn't. She has moved to an Old Peoples' Home to live, and I can't help seeing this as another sort of little death. I keep superimposing my own feelings onto the event. I think about how I'd feel if I had to leave all these possessions behind, the accumulation of a lifetime and more, some of the older items passed down from previous generations. I imagine walking out of my home for the last time, needing to say goodbye to each room as I have always done when I have left my homes.

My brother-in-law tells me she walked out without a backward glance or comment, as though she were going down to the shops and would be back in an hour's time. My sister describes her as being "as good as gold" and "like the new girl at school." I think to myself that she wants to see it this way because she master (person) minded the whole operation.

The house is not my family childhood home. She left there when my father died, when I was twelve. I left the house in the same way my father died and left my life. I went to boarding school one term and returned for the holidays to no father and a different house. No opportunities for goodbyes in either case.

This is the third house since then but I still have memories here. My now estranged husband and I lived here for three months after my daughter was born. My mother enjoyed having a small baby in the house and was more gentle and friendly than she had ever been, before or since. My daughter often stayed here with her when she was younger because I was working or studying.

She is here today, nearly sixteen, in jeans and with flowing, lion's mane hair, putting her arm around me occasionally and mumbling to me about what is going on in this unnatural, fraught-with-the-past occasion.

We have, all three of us, brought our partners, husbands in their cases and a newer love in mine. My daughter and a son-in-law of one sister are here too, but they are less involved in this age-old battle of the cradle.

We are an odd threesome, never very close, big gaps in our ages and rarely meeting except at these occasion-marking events, weddings, christenings and funerals. There are old feuds rumbling close to the surface, someone's acquisitive nature, questions of money and where has the copper kettle disappeared to. There are a number of things we mustn't mention today in order to allow the proceedings to run as smoothly as possible: politics, feminism, only children, the new Social Security Regulations, unemployment, and where have all the family photographs gone.

I want items that remind me of my childhood, a Victorian fire screen, two vases and a tiny armchair we all sat in as children. People are saying, "Does anyone want this?" in a polite, loaded way. There are memories attached to so many of these objects. I hover over some napkin rings made with tiny rows of coloured beads like Indian jewelry. It is still as familiar to my fingers as it was when I was seven. I mustn't have too much, I am a hoarder and my new love hates clutter. I can squeeze some things into my study which is my own space. I take a brass candlestick, a little dish, a plate, one of those napkin rings, and a green soup pot with a lid which we always used as children. I am surprised and pleased that we all have a pang of memory about the soup pots and take one each.

My elder sister and I keep finding presents we have given our mother over the years, a red vase, a carefully made wooden box from school days with her initials painted on, and little tiles from a school trip to Holland. We feel oddly rejected and tell each other we are being silly, she undoubtedly can't remember who gave her what or when. She forgot we were taking her out on Mother's Day and can't remember the names of our children and grandchildren.

I am haunted by something my eldest sister says as we walk home from the pub at lunchtime. I say that I had tried to talk to mother about how she felt about going into a home. My sister says she leaves all that sort of social work talk to me. She then tells me that, a little while ago, my mother said she didn't want to go. My sister told her firmly that she would have to, what were the choices, she had burnt three saucepans and left the gas on so the time had come. I say nothing, cowardly, a larger abyss forming between us.

I feel a real pang as her old brown teapot, her kitchen cutlery, and all the pottery she made in years of classes go into boxes for the Save the Children car boot sale. The irony does not escape me: who can save us grown up children now?

I start crying as I write about the old brown teapot, here in my own familiar room the same evening. My mother's possessions have fitted in around my house, the napkin ring on my desk and the cat already asleep in the tiny armchair, purring when I touch him, both of us pleased. My daughter is washing my old school trunk, wiping away my last chalk mark saying PLA, passenger's luggage in advance, and tearing off the Poole to Lyndhurst sticker. My love is cooking us a feast of sea bream and playing Miles Davis. I can go downstairs at any time and rejoin the land of the living.

I stay a little longer and look at a photo of my mother. She is about three years old and has very blonde curly hair with a fringe. She is very pretty in sepia and has what looks like a grown-up pearl necklace round her neck. She looks naked, with some gauzy material wound loosely around her, below her nipples. Her hand is lying on a large, old-fashioned childrens' picture book, but she's looking away into the distance in a dream. I wonder what she's thinking about, then and now.

Footnote: My mother died two years and a week after this piece was written. She never really adjusted to living in the Home and became increasingly senile as the time passed.

MAKING MAGGIE

Genevieve Obert

Rick's body is coated with sweat. It drips and mingles with mine, making a mess of the sheets. He's limp and panting, playing dead, while I scour his skin with my fingertips, yanking the hairs that grow about his nipples, tickling the terraced landscape of his stomach. We're done, he's exhausted, but I'm awake and goofing off.

"Sure you don't wanta try again?"

He groans, but the corners of his mouth are peaked, suppressing a smirk. Half-asleep, in mock exasperation, he grumbles. "If I'd known you'd be this horny making a baby I'd've tossed out your diaphragm years ago."

"Hah!" I slap him insolently, the impact of my palm on his wet skin the echo of a belly-flopped dive. "If you had, you'd be dead meat, sucka!" I roll clumsily over him, snatch my pillow from under his shoulder. He's already snoring, but I'm wild-eyed and happy. It's done. I can feel those slimy little suckers now. One of 'em's gonna make it this time. Some macho little polywog named Joe. Joe cool, Joe sperm.

Joe makes it all right. He grows and grows; my face glows and glows. Thinking Dr. Seuss thoughts, and Sendak wild things, and Bobby McFerrin doop-dee-doos. Now and then I get serious about this pregnancy bit. I count up the milligrams in my vitamins, I avoid smokers. I puke a lot. I don't move too fast, and I grouse. But I still have my goofy smile—the one I had that night, finger-skiing on my lover's sweat.

I puke some more. Oh man, oh man. Be good, Joe. Be nice. I'm amazed at the mass of flesh popping out in front of me, completely improbable, those bony ribs and angular hips still jutting out around this self-inflating volley ball. Big juicy purple stretch marks etch elaborate designs into my skin. It's hot, summer, I'm eight months pregnant. I put on my eeny-weeny bikini. I crack open the bedroom door.

"Oh, Rick, honey? Can you come here for a minute?"

When he opens the door I put one hand on my hip, the other on my hair, model style. Rick's in shock, but I'm laughing so hard I fall over. I bowl him over. Now he's laughing and hanging on to me as we roll on the floor. My belly feels like a big rubber ball, like it's gonna pop, and Joe's gonna bounce right out, roll out the door like the meatball in the song. I'm still laughing when Rick shuts me up with a big-mouthed kiss.

Joe's doing somersaults. He's very athletic. Feel that? That's a foot; it's working up under my rib here. See, he positions himself just so, then…wait a minute, be patient…there, watch: end over end. Thump squish thump. Volley balls don't move like that, even semi-inflated ones. I guess it really is a baby.

Good hips, my doctor says. Lots of room. No problem. Ah, but Joe's a lazy sucker. Half-hearted contractions, more than two weeks late. Come on, Joe. I might still be smiling, I'm not sure. I'm listening to inane percussive music with de-dump-dee-dumps three or four times per second: infant heart beats. They say it eases the pain; it's good for the baby. It really is inane, but it's hypnotized me, so I don't really know if I'm smiling or not.

Eight minutes apart: still lazy. Let's give him a nudge. My doctor's a small powerful woman. She laughs a lot. She's making a joke. There's a long metal prong in her hand. "See, it's just a big crochet hook. One little stitch." She breaks my water. Warm goo all over my legs, the floor. "Now maybe Joe will get the hint."

I'm sound asleep. Eight minutes of intense, deep sleep, complete with dreams of soft pillows and floating sheep. Then I wake up for one of Joe's half-hearted attempts at departure. On again off again for what—two days? I've lost track. The doctor's back. There's an amazing mass of machinery. I'm a marionette dangling from IV wires, fetal monitors, the hot hand of a very frightened Rick. The hand brings me out of my stupor. The hand is shaking. "What's…" I begin, but the Pitocin kicks in with a whammo, hallucinogenic arcs appear on graph paper. Mount Vesuvius erupts, my back arches, my ears ring with screams. It's over and then whammo, Mount Etna this time or some other mountain, somebody else's mountain; this can't be Joe talking, not my lazy Joe. It's over and then whammo...

The doctors and nurses discuss my blips and graphs in serious tones. It isn't working, mass machinery and all. Little red warning lights blink as the mountains taper into hillocks. Every eight minutes Joe reminds me he's still there with a sweetly painful scrinching on the lava plain of my belly. The red light is steady now; there's an annoying electronic beep. My doctor screams at the nurses, disconnects the wires. I'm rolled heavily onto a gurney.

Somehow I sleep again, and Grandma is there, feverishly mixing. German chocolate cake, my favorite. She hands me the bowl, "Your turn!" My hand grips the spoon and freezes. The bowl is filled with concrete. Grandma laughs in her gravelly voice.

I wake with a start and the lights are too bright. The doctors are calmer. They're standing around in blue paper suits and hats and gloves, waiting for something. A blue-masked man keeps tapping my thigh with cold wet cotton balls and asking "Do you feel that?" and I say "Yes." Another dribble of icy fluid down my spine, then he asks again, "Can you feel this?" and I say "Yes." A blue paper wall goes up, cutting me in half. Now the voices have no faces. There's mumbling, more cold taps with cotton balls. I keep saying yes. My doctor says "We can't wait." I say—maybe I scream—"I can still feel it!" but then hot hot slicing and slicing—like scoring a thick piece of cardboard over and over so you can bend it—slicing again through all the layers—it isn't my skin anymore, it's some sort of buttery leather, like a fine Italian jacket with extra layers of lining beneath. And the heat, like a knife dipped in hot fluid to make it slice through smoothly...Then my doctor's small strong hands push at the leather walls, my belly, my gut, pull me apart, no hot butter to smooth it, just a scrunching rip, squishing all my innards out. My throat is raw, my ears are ringing. Rick squeezes my hand. I see his face, green in the blue light. He might throw up. The mass of pain rolls in waves down my legs. I'm deflating, a weight is lifting. And the voices— no cry from the baby, where is the baby?—I hear my doctor say,

"Oh my God, look at all this meconium! Clear all this out of here."
I see two hands reach in me and scoop out dripping gobs of black
and green goo. The baby pooped too soon. It's dripping through
my doctor's fingers in my head. I can't see or hear or feel—only
ice cold dribbles down my spine and the cotton ball guy saying,
"You'll feel better now."

A strangely calm terror invades my drugged sleep. I know the
baby's dead. I messed up. I didn't pay attention. I never take
things seriously. I never want to wake up: I have no body, no baby.
But then Grandma shows up again, shaking me awake.

"Honey, you've been out for hours. Are you ok?"

It's Rick. I can't talk. I'm devastated. I see my arm extend,
grab the hair behind his ear, pull his face onto mine. Coffee breath,
unshaven skin. I try my voice. "I'm sorry" comes out, barely a
whisper. He looks at me puzzled, that satisfied smile on his face.

He steps aside and I see. A nurse fiddles with a swaddled
bundle inside a clear plastic box. She untangles a mass of wires,
lifts the bundle and sets it down beside me. A tiny ancient face
stares up at me: an apple doll Queen Victoria. No smiles or signs
of recognition, but steel blue eyes stare. I touch the fine brown
hair, the hands, the toes, and spin a web around us, sticking us
together, fine as silk, strong as metal. No one can cut it. Rick
reaches in, pushing aside the threads, gently rests his hand upon
mine upon hers. The sticky web stretches, but does not break. He
leans down into the web. His laughing eyes are proud.

"You were wrong, honey. It's not a boy. What'll we call her?
We can't call her Joe…"

I try my voice again, but I'm not sure if he hears.

Awhile later, my wrist wears a new name, Grandma's name.
In the clear plastic crib next to my bed, the little girl watches me.
We're alone in the dusk-lit room.

"Hello, Maggie." My voice is clearer now.

In slow motion she blinks. Tiny vibrations, miniature sound
waves, the voices of an old woman and a young child. They flutter
across the web.

When her eyes close again, I remember how to breathe.

FOREST KISS

Ellen A. Kelley

I know why the alpine stream's
trickled ice water
squirting from the boulder
surprised me
hidden between moss and tender violet
subtly encased
its water voice startled
then charmed
my animal memory
seduced the far, furry heart
told me this was
a place plucked from dreams
sent to Earth for the moment
door of instinct
flesh of my past
terrifying cradle of my longing
and I was certain
it gave the deer and unicorn
their nightly drink
and I leaned over the rock
opened the secret of the stream
gushing full in mouth
as my lips felt the spot
where forest creatures curved
their own thirsty mouths.
So in drinking had I
kissed the beasts
and was more they
than myself

THE WRITER

D. Nico Leto

her face
a sculptors dream
her work
an architecture of
string and people's conversations
her hair turns others
but it is her art
that moves me
words in and out
of every little place
if her smile
could tell stories
whole civilizations
would fall
with the news

CONTRIBUTORS

Catharine Clark-Sayles is a physician practicing internal medicine and geriatrics in Mill Valley, CA. She considers herself one of the lucky people in life who gets to do something she loves. Having left poetry behind in college and medical training, she returned to writing when she turned forty last year. She has had a poem accepted by the *Western Journal of Medicine*. Although she rejoices in life, many of her poems are about death and illness, the inevitable consequence of taking care of so many people at the end of their lives. Writing about them provides comfort and catharsis.

Gloria Dyc's poetry and fiction have been published in numerous small press journals, most recently *yefief* and *Short Fiction by Women*. She teaches English and communication courses at the University of New Mexico-Gallup Campus. For ten years, she worked with the *Moving Out* collective in Detroit; the first issue of this Feminist Literary Journal was published in 1969.

Vesna Dye is an American Yugoslav writer born in Zagreb, Croatia, and living in Santa Cruz, CA, for the last 14 years. She has been published in small magazines in Yugoslavia and USA. Her first book is to be published in the fall of 1994 by University Editions of West Virginia. "Backpacking Through Illusions," is a fictionalized autobiography of her year in Australia, remembering her native Yugoslavia. It could be the story of any solitary, artistic immigrant woman in her late 30's without a permanent home and afraid of aging.

Alethea Eason will see one of her poems published in the anthology *Poems: From Prayers to Protest* some time in 1995. She is currently working on a historical/fantasy novel for middle grade readers set on the Klamath River.

Christine Gallegos began writing seventeen years ago during a period of extreme anxiety. The anxiety has subsided; the writing has continued. Her childhood years were years of abuse, neglect and disassociation. Her young marriage was to an alcoholic who has since reformed. She began to know herself through her writing and look for ways to feed her soul, learn and grow into herself.

Vanessa Gang's writing has appeared in *Splinters*, *Recovery*, and *Columbia University's School of Nursing Alumnae Magazine*. She reads her poetry regularly at An Bael Bacht in New York City.

Leonne Gould, born in 1937, is an "old" English teacher and an even older dance teacher finally publishing poetry. She teaches at Deep Creek Middle School in Baltimore and writes, dances, canoes, photographs, loves her kids and plays as much as possible.

Tova Green is a San Francisco Bay Area activist and writer. She visited the former Yugoslavia three times in 1993-94. She is the author of *Insight and Action: How to Discern and Sustain a Life of Integrity and Change* (New Society Publishers, 1994).

Cora Greenhill lives in Derbyshire, central England, among the ancient hills and sacred circles of her ancestors. The landscape is sustaining her through the difficult dances of mid-life, and she's still dancing! She is finishing her first novel set in ancient and modern Crete: another spiritual homeland. Her collection, *Dreadful Work*, is still available from her.

Lee Anne Grundish has a B.A. in Psychology, and is self employed as a career counselor, working primarily with women, in issues of self empowerment and success. She is an artist, with a jewelry design business. While she has been writing poetry virtually her whole life, she has only recently begun seeking publication and, to date, has published 45 pieces in 16 publications throughout the U.S. and Canada.

Monica Gunning was born in Jamaica, West Indies. While teaching in the United States, she developed a love of children's literature and a desire to write for youngsters. She is the author of the picture books *Perico Bonito*, a bilingual book, *The Two Georges*, and *Not a Copper Penny in Me House*.

Jill Hammer is a poet who involves herself in women's learning and spirituality. She is pursuing a doctorate in social psychology at the University of Connecticut and will attend rabbinical school at the Jewish Theology Seminary in 1995. Her poems have been published in *Response*, *Encodings*, *Voices Israel*, *Point Judith Light* and *Sunflower*. She lives with her husband in Middletown, CT.

Nancy Harvey lives in New Hampshire where she teaches writing at New England college. She would like to thank her mentor, Tamar March, and her friend, Fran Chelland, for forcing her to finally send her poems out into the world.

Margaret Hehman-Smith received an MFA in 1975 (BFA 1973) from Otis Art Institute, Los Angeles, CA, in painting and printmaking. Since 1988 she has had numerous articles published as a freelance writer. She has just finished her first novel, a story about baboons. Her late husband was a noted animal behaviorist.

Christine Irving is now in California after living since 1979 in Saudi Arabia with her husband of 27 years, who is a pilot. While her first love is poetry, she has also written travel articles, an unpublished book, and chapter books for children. She alternates between writing and working in paper collage, recycling images into new compositions. A long-time feminist, deeply responsive to women's spirituality, she finds her poetry moving toward the expression of spiritual intuitions and insights, reflecting her personal growth as she evolves through middle-age. She wrote this poem as a birthday gift for a friend.

Irene Keenan is a freelance writer who resides in California with her husband and two children.

Ellen A. Kelley. Writing always felt familiar to her, even as a child. She's been writing adult poetry and children's fiction for nine years. Writing poems makes you dig deep. If you're lucky, you hit the real stuff. "Forest Kiss" is a true story. She was 11.

Denise Nico Leto is a poet living in Oakland, CA, with her partner Mary, their Great Dane, Baily, and two cats, Bopper and Macaroni. Her work has appeared in many publications, most recently by Penguin in *Unsettling America: An*

Anthology of Contemporary Multicultural Poetry.

maryellen's life journey has continued, and with great personal cost as well as with the joy of discovering and being herself, she has come to a better place. She is now an ordained minister, healthcare administrator, and author. She continues to advocate for women in abusive relationships.

Nancy McGovern grew up on a ranch on the Mexican border. She's an ASU graduate in English-Spanish. Having been a teacher, social worker, and roofing company owner, she is presently a market research interviewer and works in connection with homes for abused children. She has six cats and four dogs and is an environmentalist.

Juliana Neely is thirteen years old and in eighth grade. Her poem "Grandma" won first prize in the junior division of the 68th Annual Poets Dinner in Berkeley, CA, March, 1994. She had another poem entitled "Puppy" published in the *Anthology of Poets by Young Americans.*

Lian Njo was born and raised in Indonesia. In 1966 she immigrated to the USA. In additiion to writing poetry she writes short stories. Currently she is working on a novel using the Dutch colonialism and the Indonesian revolution as a backdrop. "Co-dependent" is her first published poem.

Renee Norman is a graduate student in the English Education Department at the University of British Columbia and teaches part-time in Vancouver school district. She is the mother of three daughters, aged five, eight and ten and is committed to writing about women's lives and issues. Her poetry has been published in *Contemporary Verse 2, Prairie Journal, Common Ground* and *English Quarterly.* She also free lance writes for the *Vancouver Sun* newspaper.

Genevieve Obert was possessed by writing after the birth of her first child. She now has two small children, and spends the late-night hours finishing her first mystery novel.

Fran Peavy is a teacher, comedian, author and social change catalyst on the international and community levels. She toured internationally as an Atomic Comic. Her books include *Heart Politics, A Shallow Pool of Time,* and recently, *By Life's Grace: Musings on the Essence of Social Change.* Her work has taken her from San Francisco to India, South Africa, and the former Yugoslavia, grappling with the issues of our time.

Judy Powell lives and writes in Memphis, Tennessee.

Jean Pumphrey teaches poetry and creative writing at the College of San Mateo, California, where she founded the CSM Poetry Center. Author of *Poetry: The Way Through Language,* Harper & Row, and *Sheltered at the Edge,* Solo Press, her poem "San Miguel" was awarded highest commendation and published in *International Who's Who in Poetry,* London.

Gwendolyn Raver was born in Baltimore, and currently lives in New York. She is completing a doctorate in Ancient History and works as a consultant at the New York Historical Society. She is also working on a biography on E.G. Squire and trying to finish a novel about a Western Maryland family.

Sally Reeves works as a free lance writer and as a social worker in a hospice for terminally ill cancer patients. She has had a number of articles, mainly on travel, published in magazines, but has recently been concentrating on writing short stories. She lives in Southampton, England, with her partner and two black cats, Miles and Blakey. She has a daughter Victoria and granddaughter Aurelia.

Rhiannon is a prominent San Francisco Bay Area teacher of voice and improvisation for creative artists. Following a lifetime's experience as actor, director and singer, in recent years she's broken new ground as an acclaimed solo jazz story-teller—a unique combination of song, story, movement and the unexpected. She's created two performance pieces: *Toward Home* (on CD) and *Bowl Full of Sound*. Currently she is working internationally bringing music and improvisation into the realm of social change.

Priscilla Rhoades makes her living as a fundraiser for a non-profit health organization. She describes her personal history as just a little weirder than The X Files. A recent auric reading by a friendly psychic told her she was among the violet people here to save the planet. We'll see, she says.

Brooke Silverbrand is fifteen years old, in tenth grade at Clarkstown North High School, in New York state. She belongs to many different after school activities, including the Spanish Club, Crafts Club and Candle. She has many interests such as playing the piano and tennis.

Charlene Mary-Cath Smith is an art museum docent…practically punctuationless poet with an affinity for minimalist work not only for its obvious ability to utilize more of less but simply for its (subjective) aesthetic appeal upon the white of its page. She has enjoyed/appreciated placement of 200 poems in varied publications in USA, UK, Canada, India.

Mia T. Starr was born in Vietnam and immigrated to America in 1975. In 1992, she graduated from the University of Michigan, and is currently working and living in New York City. She has been writing poetry not only to express herself, but hopefully to share some insights and truths about how she sees the world we live in.

Crystal Stone is a writer/artist living in the Highland, IN, area. Her works, both writing and art, lean towards reflecting on and recognizing and understanding human frailties. She is married and has a daughter, 23.

Eileen Storey successfully escaped southeast Texas to reside for the next couple years in rural Japan, where she is an Assistant English Teacher. She enjoys teaching slang to her students, and hopes to learn enough Japanese to be able to write poetry in the language. She really misses cheddar cheese.

Theano Storm was born in Boston, October 27, 1939, "a stranger in a strange land"—a scorpio—destined to experience death/rebirth, depression/elation, loss/gifts…. This poem, "Grieving…," is but one of a flood that began the fourth day after her son left his body—and ever so slowly, subsided…

B.J. Swan credits the birth of any creativity gene(s) to her move to California from the Florida Keys. Now residing and writing in Mountain View, CA, she is a former Peace Corps volunteer, an avid biker, and currently a biotech librarian. This first acceptance brings joy and excitement.

SUBSCRIPTION FORM

	U.S.	Canada/ Mexico	Overseas (includes airmail)
single copy rates:	$ 6.00	$ 6.25	$ 8.00
subscription rates, two issues:	$11.50	$12.00	$15.50
1992 back issues:	$ 4.00	$ 4.25	$ 6.00

Please send me a **subscription** for

☐ 1 year (2 issues) $ _____

☐ 2 years (4 issues) $ _____

New_____ Renew_____

Start with: current issue_____ next issue_____

Please send me the following **single issues:**

V1n1(92)____V1n2(92)_____V2n1(93)_____

V2n2(94)____V3n1(94)_____V3n2(95)_____ $ _____

Please send a **gift subscription** to

Name_____

Street address_____

City, State, Zip_____

Country_____ $ _____

    In California add 8.25% **sales tax** $ _____

In North America please help by contributing

$1.00 shipping/handling per copy $ _____

I have enclosed my check or money order for **$** _____

payable to **Running Deer Press**

Your name_____

Street address_____

City, State, Zip_____

Country_____ Phone_____

Send completed form to **Running Deer Press,
647 N. Santa Cruz Ave., ANNEX, Los Gatos, CA 95030.**

Help support women's creative expressions in writing. *Writing For Our Lives* is a privately funded labor of love. Additional contributions gratefully accepted.